Book 1
Android Programming In a Day!

BY SAM KEY

&

Book 2
PHP Programming Professional Made Easy

BY SAM KEY

Book 1
Android Programming In a Day!

BY SAM KEY

The Power Guide for Beginners In Android App Programming

Programming Box Set #81: Android Programming in a Day & PHP Programming Professional Made Easy

Table Of Contents

Introduction

I want to thank you and congratulate you for purchasing the book, "Introduction to Android Programming in a Day – The Power Guide for Beginners in Android App Programming".

This book contains proven steps and strategies on how to get started with Android app development.

This book will focus on preparing you with the fun and tiring world of Android app development. Take note that this book will not teach you on how to program. It will revolve around the familiarization of the Android SDK and Eclipse IDE.

Why not focus on programming immediately? Unfortunately, the biggest reason many aspiring Android developers stop on learning this craft is due to the lack of wisdom on the Android SDK and Eclipse IDE.

Sure, you can also make apps using other languages like Python and other IDEs on the market. However, you can expect that it is much more difficult than learning Android's SDK and Eclipse's IDE.

On the other hand, you can use tools online to develop your Android app for you. But where's the fun in that? You will not learn if you use such tools. Although it does not mean that you should completely stay away from that option.

Anyway, the book will be split into four chapters. The first will prepare you and tell you the things you need before you develop apps. The second will tell you how you can configure your project. The third will introduce you to the Eclipse IDE. And the last chapter will teach you on how to run your program in your Android device.

Also, this book will be sprinkled with tidbits about the basic concepts of Android app development. And as you read along, you will have an idea on what to do next.

Thanks again for purchasing this book, I hope you enjoy it!

Chapter 1: Preparation

Android application development is not easy. You must have some decent background in program development. It is a plus if you know Visual Basic and Java. And it will be definitely a great advantage if you are familiar or have already used Eclipse's IDE (Integrated Development Environment). Also, being familiar with XML will help you.

You will need a couple of things before you can start developing apps.

First, you will need a high-end computer. It is common that other programming development kits do not need a powerful computer in order to create applications. However, creating programs for Android is a bit different. You will need more computing power for you to run Android emulators, which are programs that can allow you to test your programs in your computer.

Using a weak computer without a decent processor and a good amount of RAM will only make it difficult for you to run those emulators. If you were able to run it, it will run slowly.

Second, you will need an Android device. That device will be your beta tester. With it, you will know how your program will behave in an Android device. When choosing the test device, make sure that it is at par with the devices of the market you are targeting for your app. If you are targeting tablet users, use a tablet. If you are targeting smartphones, then use a smartphone.

Third, you will need the Android SDK (Software Development Kit) from Google. The SDK is a set of files and programs that can allow you to create and compile your program's code. As of this writing, the latest Android SDK's file size is around 350mb. It will take you 15 – 30 minutes to download it. If you uncompressed the Android SDK file, it will take up around 450mb of your computer's disk space. The link to the download page is: http://developer.android.com/sdk/index.html

The SDK can run on Windows XP, Windows 7, Mac OSX 10.8.5 (or higher), and Linux distros that can run 32bit applications and has glibc (GNU C library) 2.11 or higher.

Once you have unpacked the contents of the file you downloaded, open the SDK Manager. That program is the development kit's update tool. To make sure you have the latest versions of the kit's components, run the manager once in a while and download those updates. Also, you can use the SDK Manager to download older versions of SDK. You must do that in case you want to make programs with devices with dated Android operating systems.

Chapter 2: Starting Your First Project

To start creating programs, you will need to open Eclipse. The Eclipse application file can be found under the eclipse folder on the extracted files from the Android SDK. Whenever you run Eclipse, it will ask you where you want your Eclipse workspace will be stored. You can just use the default location and just toggle the don't show checkbox.

New Project

To start a new Android application project, just click on the dropdown button of the New button on Eclipse's toolbar. A context menu will appear, and click on the Android application project.

The New Android Application project details window will appear. In there, you will need to input some information for your project. You must provide your program's application name, project name, and package name. Also, you can configure the minimum and target SDK where your program can run and the SDK that will be used to compile your code. And lastly, you can indicate the default theme that your program will use.

Application Name

The application name will be the name that will be displayed on the Google's Play Store when you post it there. The project name will be more of a file name for Eclipse. It will be the project's identifier. It should be unique for every project that you build in Eclipse. By default, Eclipse will generate a project and package name for your project when you type something in the Application Name text box.

Package Name

The package name is not usually displayed for users. Take note that in case you will develop a large program, you must remember that your package name should never be changed. On the other hand, it is common that package names are the reverse of your domain name plus your project's name. For example, if your website's domain name is www.mywebsite.com and your project's name is Hello World, a good package name for your project will be com.mywebsite.helloworld.

The package name should follow the Java package name convention. The naming convention is there to prevent users from having similar names, which could result to numerous conflicts. Some of the rules you need to follow for the package name are:

- Your package name should be all in lower caps. Though Eclipse will accept a package name with a capital letter, but it is still best to adhere to standard practice.
- The reverse domain naming convention is included as a standard practice.
- Avoid using special characters in the package name. Instead, you can replace it with underscores.
- Also, you should never use or include the default com.example in your package name. Google Play will not accept an app with a package name like that.

Minimum SDK

Minimum required SDK could be set to lower or the lowest version of Android. Anything between the latest and the set minimum required version can run your program. Setting it to the lowest, which is API 1 or Android 1.0, can make your target audience wider.

Setting it to Android 2.2 (Froyo) or API 8, can make your program run on almost 95% of all Android devices in the world. The drawback fn this is that the features you can include in your program will be limited. Adding new features will force your minimum required SDK to move higher since some of the new functions in Android is not available on lower versions of the API (Application Programming Interface).

Target SDK

The target SDK should be set to the version of Android that most of your target audience uses. It indicates that you have tested your program to that version. And it means that your program is fully functional if they use it on a device that runs the target Android version.

Whenever a new version of Android appears, you should also update the target SDK of your program. Of course, before you release it to the market again, make sure that you test it on an updated device.

If a device with the same version as your set target SDK runs your program, it will not do any compatibility behavior or adjust itself to run the program. By default, you should set it to the highest version to attract your potential app buyers. Setting a lower version for your target SDK would make your program old and dated. By the way, the target SDK should be always higher or equal with the minimum target SDK version.

Compile with

The compile with version should be set to the latest version of Android. This is to make sure that your program will run on almost all versions down to the minimum version you have indicated, and to take advantage of the newest features and optimization offered by the latest version of Android. By default, the Android SDK will only have one version available for this option, which is API 20 or Android 4.4 (KitKat Wear).

After setting those all up, it is time to click on the Next button. The new page in the screen will contain some options such as creating custom launcher icon and creating activity. As of now, you do not need to worry about those. Just leave the default values and check, and click the Next button once again.

Custom Launcher Icon

Since you have left the Create Custom Launcher option checked, the next page will bring you in the launcher icon customization page. In there, you will be given three options on how you would create your launcher. Those options are launcher icons made from an image, clipart, or text.

With the text and clipart method, you can easily create an icon you want without thinking about the size and quality of the launcher icon. With those two, you can just get a preset image from the SDK or Android to use as a launcher icon. The same goes with the text method since all you need is to type the letters you want to appear on the icon and the SDK will generate an icon based on that.

The launcher icon editor also allows you to change the background and foreground color of your icon. Also, you can scale the text and clipart by changing the value of the additional padding of the icon. And finally, you can add simple 3D shapes on your icon to make it appear more professional.

Bitmap Iconography Tips

When it comes to images, you need to take note of a few reminders. First, always make sure that you will use vector images. Unlike the typical bitmap images (pictures taken from cameras or images created using Paint), vector images provide accurate and sharp images. You can scale it multiple times, but its sharpness will not disappear and will not pixelate. After all, vector images do not contain information about pixels. It only has numbers and location of the colors and lines that will appear in it. When it is scaled, it does not perform antialiasing or stretching since its image will be mathematically rendered.

In case that you will be the one creating or designing the image that you will use for your program and you will be creating a bitmap image, make sure that you start with a large image. A large image is easier to create and design.

Also, since in Android, multiple sizes of your icon will be needed, a large icon can make it easier for you to make smaller ones. Take note that if you scale a big picture into a small one, some details will be lost, but it will be easier to edit and fix and it will still look crisp. On the other hand, if you scale a small image into a big one, it will pixelate and insert details that you do not intend to show such as jagged and blurred edges.

Nevertheless, even when scaling down a big image into a smaller one, do not forget to rework the image. Remember that a poor-looking icon makes people think that the app you are selling is low-quality. And again, if you do not want to go through all that, create a vector image instead.

Also, when you create an image, make sure that it will be visible in any background. Aside from that, it is advisable to make it appear uniform with other Android icons. To do that, make sure that your image has a distinct silhouette that will make it look like a 3D image. The icon should appear as if you were looking above it and as if the source of light is on top of the image. The topmost part of the icon should appear lighter and the bottom part should appear darker.

Activity

Once you are done with your icon, click on the Next button. The page will now show the Activity window. It will provide you with activity templates to work on. The window has a preview box where you can see what your app will look like for every activity template. Below the selection, there is a description box that will tell you what each template does. For now, select the Blank Activity and click Next. The next page will ask you some details regarding the activity. Leave it on its default values and click Finish.

Once you do that, Eclipse will setup your new project. It might take a lot of time, especially if you are using a dated computer. The next chapter will discuss the programming interface of Eclipse.

Chapter 3: Getting Familiar with Eclipse and Contents of an Android App

When Eclipse has finished its preparation, you will be able to start doing something to your program. But hold onto your horses; explore Eclipse first before you start fiddling with anything.

Editing Area

In the middle of the screen, you will see a preview of your program. In it, you will see your program's icon beside the title of your program. Just left of it is the palette window. It contains all the elements that you can place in your program.

Both of these windows are inside Eclipse's editing area. You will be spending most of your time here, especially if you are going to edit or view something in your code or layout.

The form widgets tab will be expanded in the palette by default. There you will see the regular things you see in an Android app such as buttons, radio buttons, progress bar (the circle icon that spins when something is loading in your device or the bar the fills up when your device is loading), seek bar, and the ratings bar (the stars you see in reviews).

Aside from the form widgets, there are other elements that you can check and use. Press the horizontal tabs or buttons and examine all the elements you can possibly use in your program.

To insert a widget in your program, you can just drag the element you want to include from the palette and drop it in your program's preview. Eclipse will provide you visual markers and grid snaps for you to place the widgets you want on the exact place you want. Easy, right?

Take note, some of the widgets on the palette may require higher-level APIs or versions of Android. For example, the Grid Layout from the Layouts section of the palette requires API 14 (Android 4.0 Ice Cream Sandwich) or higher. If you add it in your program, it will ask you if you want to install it. In case you did include and install it, remember that it will not be compatible for older versions or any device running on API 13 and lower. It is advisable that you do not include any element that asks for installation. It might result into errors.

Output Area, Status Bar, and Problem Browser

On the bottom part of Eclipse, the status bar, problem browser, and output area can be found. It will contain messages regarding to the state of your project. If Eclipse found errors in your program, it will be listed there. Always check the Problems bar for any issues. Take note that you cannot run or compile your program if Eclipse finds at least one error on your project.

Navigation Pane

On the leftmost part of your screen is the navigation pane that contains the package explorer. The package explorer lets you browse all the files that are included in your project. Three of the most important files that you should know where to look for are:

- activity_main.xml: This file is your program's main page or window. And it will be the initial file that will be opened when you create a new project. In case you accidentally close it on your editor window, you can find it at: YourProjectName > res > layout > activity_main.xml.

- MainActivity.java: As of now, you will not need to touch this file. However, it is important to know where it is since later in your Android development activities, you will need to understand it and its contents. It is located at: YourProjectName > src > YourPackageName > MainActivity.java.

- AndroidManifest.xml: It contains the essential information that you have set up a while ago when you were creating your project file in Eclipse. You can edit the minimum and target SDK in there. It is located at YourProjectName > AndroidManifest.xml.

Aside from those files, you should take note of the following directories:

- src/: This is where most of your program's source files will be placed. And your main activity file is locafile is located.

- res/: Most of the resources will be placed here. The resources are placed inside the subdirectories under this folder.

- res/drawable-hdpi/: Your high density bitmap files that you might show in your app will go in here.

- res/layout/: All the pages or interface in your app will be located here – including your activity_main.xml.

- res/values/: The values you will store and use in your program will be placed in this directory in form of XML files.

In the event that you will create multiple projects, remember that the directory for those other projects aside from the one you have opened will still be available in your package explorer. Because of that, you might get confused over the files you are working on. Thankfully, Eclipse's title bar indicates the location and name of the file you are editing, which makes it easier to know what is currently active on the editing area.

Outline Box

Displays the current structure of the file you are editing. The outline panel will help you visualize the flow and design of your app. Also, it can help you find the widgets you want to edit.

Properties Box

Whenever you are editing a layout file, the properties box will appear below the outline box. With the properties box, you can edit certain characteristics of a widget. For example, if you click on the Hello World text on the preview of your main activity layout file, the contents of the properties box will be populated. In there, you can edit the properties of the text element that you have clicked. You can change the text, height, width, and even its font color.

Menu and Toolbar

The menu bar contains all the major functionalities of Eclipse. In case you do not know where the button of a certain tool is located, you can just invoke that tool's function on the menu bar. On the other hand, the tool bar houses all the major functions in Eclipse. The most notable buttons there are the New, Save, and Run.

As of now, look around Eclipse's interface. Also, do not do or change anything on the main activity file or any other file. The next chapter will discuss about how to run your program. As of now, the initial contents of your project are also valid as an android program. Do not change anything since you might produce an unexpected error. Nevertheless, if you really do want to change something, go ahead. You can just create another project for you to keep up with the next chapter.

Chapter 4: Running Your Program

By this time, even if you have not done anything yet to your program, you can already run and test it in your Android device or emulator. Why teach this first before the actual programming? Well, unlike typical computer program development, Android app development is a bit bothersome when it comes to testing.

First, the program that you are developing is intended for Android devices. You cannot actually run it normally in your computer without the help of an emulator. And you will actually do a lot of testing. Even with the first lines of code or changes in your program, you will surely want to test it.

Second, the Android emulator works slow. Even with good computers, the emulator that comes with the Android SDK is painstakingly sluggish. Alternatively, you can use BlueStacks. BlueStacks is a free Android emulator that works better than the SDK's emulator. It can even run games with it! However, it is buggy and does not work well (and does not even run sometimes) with every computer.

This chapter will focus on running your program into your Android device. You will need to have a USB data cable and connect your computer and Android. Also, you will need to have the right drivers for your device to work as a testing platform for the programs you will develop. Unfortunately, this is the preferred method for most beginners since running your app on Android emulators can bring a lot more trouble since it is super slow. And that might even discourage you to continue Android app development.

Why Android Emulators are Slow

Why are Android emulators slow? Computers can run virtual OSs without any problems, but why cannot the Android emulator work fine? Running virtual OSs is not something as resource-extensive anymore with today's computer standards. However, with Android, you will actually emulate an OS together with a mobile device. And nowadays, these mobile devices are as powerful as some of the dated computers back then. Regular computers will definitely have a hard time with that kind of payload from an Android emulator.

USB Debugging Mode

To run your program in an Android device, connect your Android to your computer. After that, set your Android into USB debugging mode. Depending on the version of the Android device you are using, the steps might change.

For 3.2 and older Android devices:

Go to Settings > Applications > Development

For 4.0 and newer Android devices:

Go to Settings > Developer Options

For 4.2 and newer Android devices with hidden Developer Options:

Go to Settings > About Phone. After that, tap the Build Number seven times. Go back to the previous screen. The Developer Options should be visible now.

Android Device Drivers

When USB debugging is enabled, your computer will install the right drivers for the Android device that you have. If your computer does not have the right drivers, you will not be able to run your program on your device. If that happens to you, visit this page: http://developer.android.com/tools/extras/oem-usb.html. It contains instructions on how you can install the right driver for your device and operating system.

Running an App in Your Android Device Using Eclipse

Once your device is already connected and you have the right drivers for it, you can now do a test run of your application. On your Eclipse window, click the Run button on the toolbar or in the menu bar.

If a Run As window appeared, select the Android Application option and click on the OK button. After that, a dialog box will appear. It will provide you with two options: running the program on an Android device or on an AVD (Android Virtual Device) or emulator.

If your device was properly identified by your computer, it will appear on the list. Click on your device's name and click OK. Eclipse will compile your Android app, install it on your device, and then run it. That is how simple it is.

Take note, there will be times that your device will appear offline on the list. In case that happens, there are two simple fixes that you can do to make it appear online again: restart your device or disable and enable the USB debugging function on your device.

Now, you can start placing widgets on your main activity file. However, always make sure that you do not place any widgets that require higher APIs.

Conclusion

Thank you again for purchasing this book!

I hope this book was able to help you get started with Android Programming in a Day!.

The next step is to study the following:

View and Viewgroups: View and Viewgroups are the two types of objects that you will be dealing with Android. View objects are the elements or widgets that you see in Android programs. Viewgroup objects act as containers to those View objects.

Relative, Linear, and Table Layout: When it comes to designing your app, you need to know the different types of layouts. In later versions of Android, you can use other versions of layouts, but of course, the API requirements will go up if you use them. Master these, and you will be able to design faster and cleaner.

Adding Activities or Interface: Of course, you would not want your program to contain one page only. You need more. You must let your app customers to see more content and functions. In order to do that, you will need to learn adding activities to your program. This is the part when developing your Android app will be tricky. You will not be able to rely completely on the drag and drop function and graphical layout view of Eclipse. You will need to start typing some code into your program.

Adding the Action Bar: The action bar is one of the most useful elements in Android apps. It provides the best location for the most used functions in your program. And it also aid your users when switching views, tabs, or drop down list.

Once you have gain knowledge on those things, you will be able to launch a decent app on the market. The last thing you might want to do is to learn how to make your program support other Android devices.

You must know very well that Android devices come in all shapes and form. An Android device can be a tablet, a smartphone, or even a television. Also, they come with different screen sizes. You cannot just expect that all your customers will be using a 4-inch display smartphone. Also, you should think about the versions of Android they are using. Lastly, you must also add language options to your programs. Even though English is fine, some users will appreciate if your program caters to the primary language that they use.

And that is about it for this book. Make sure you do not stop learning Android app development.

Finally, if you enjoyed this book, please take the time to share your thoughts and post a review on Amazon. We do our best to reach out to readers and provide the best value we can. Your positive review will help us achieve that. It'd be greatly appreciated!

Thank you and good luck!

Book 2
PHP Programming Professional Made Easy

BY SAM KEY

Expert PHP Programming Language Success in a Day for any Computer User!

Programming Box Set #81: Android Programming in a Day & PHP Programming Professional Made Easy

Table of Contents

Introduction

I want to thank you and congratulate you for purchasing the book, "Professional PHP Programming Made Easy: Expert PHP Programming Language Success in a Day for any Computer User!"

This book contains proven steps and strategies on how to quickly transition from client side scripting to server side scripting using PHP.

The book contains a condensed version of all the topics you need to know about PHP as a beginner. To make it easier for you to understand the lessons, easy to do examples are included.

If you are familiar with programming, it will only take you an hour or two to master the basics of PHP. If you are new to programming, expect that you might take two to three days to get familiar with this great server scripting language.

Thanks again for purchasing this book, I hope you enjoy it!

Chapter 1: Setting Expectations and Preparation

PHP is a scripting language primarily used by web developers to create interactive and dynamic websites. This book will assume that you are already familiar with HTML and CSS. By the way, a little bit of XML experience is a plus.

This book will also assume that you have a good understanding and experience with JavaScript since most of the explanations and examples here will use references to that client side scripting language

To be honest, this will be like a reference book to PHP that contains bits of explanations. And since JavaScript is commonly treated as a prerequisite to learning PHP, it is expected that most web developers will experience no difficulty in shifting to using this server side scripting language.

However, if you have little knowledge of JavaScript or any other programming language, expect that you will have a steep learning curve if you use this book. Nevertheless, it does not mean that it is impossible to learn PHP without a solid background in programming or client side scripting. You just need to play more with the examples presented in this book to grasp the meaning and purpose of the lessons.

Anyway, unlike JavaScript or other programming languages, you cannot just test PHP codes in your computer. You will need a server to process it for you. There are three ways to do that:

1. Get a web hosting account. Most web hosting packages available on the web are PHP ready. All you need to do is code your script, save it as .php or .htm, upload it to your web directory, and access it.

2. Make your computer as simple web server. You can do that by installing a web server application in your computer. If your computer is running on Microsoft Windows, you can install XAMPP to make your computer act like a web server. Do not worry. Your computer will be safe since your XAMPP, by default, will make your computer only available to your use.

3. Use an online source code editor that can execute PHP codes. Take note that this will be a bit restricting since most of them only accept and execute PHP codes. It means that you will not be able to mix HTML, CSS, JavaScript, and PHP in one go. But if you are going to study the basics, which the lessons in this book are all about, it will be good enough.

Chapter 2: PHP Basics

This chapter will teach you the primary things that you need to know when starting to code PHP. It includes PHP's syntax rules, variables, constants, echo and print, operators, and superglobals.

Syntax

PHP code can be placed anywhere in an HTML document or it can be saved in a file with .php as its file extension. Just like JavaScript, you will need to enclose PHP code inside tags to separate it from HTML. The tag will tell browsers that all the lines inside it are PHP code.

PHP's opening tag is <?php and its closing tag is ?>. For example:

```
<!DOCTYPE html>
</html>
<head></head>
<body>
    <h1>Heading for the page</h2>
    <p>Some paragraph</p>
    <?php
        // Insert some PHP code in here.
    ?>
</body>
</html>
```

Echo and Print

PHP code blocks do not only return the values you requested from them, but you can also let it return HTML or text to the HTML file that invoked the PHP code blocks. To do that, you will need to use the echo or print command. Below are samples on how they can be used:

```
<?php
echo “Hello World!”;
?>
<?php
print “Hello World!”;
```

```
?>
```

Once the browser parses that part of the HTML, that small code will be processed on the server, and the server will send the value “Hello World” back to the client. Browsers handle echo and print values by placing them in the HTML file code. It will appear after the HTML element where the PHP code was inserted. For example:

```
<p>This is a paragraph.</p>
<?php
echo “Hello World!”;
?>
<p>This is another paragraph.</p>
```

Once the browser parses those lines, this will be the result:

This is a paragraph.

Hello World!

This is another paragraph.

You can even echo HTML elements. For example:

```
<p>P1.</p>
<?php
print “<a href=’http://www.google.com’ >Google</a>”;
?>
<p>P2.</p>
```

As you have witnessed, both echo and print have identical primary function, which is to send output to the browser. They have two differences however. Print can only handle one parameter while echo can handle multiple parameters. Another difference is that you can use print in expressions since it returns a value of 1 while you cannot use echo. Below is a demonstration of their differences:

```
<?php
echo “Hello World!”, “How are you?”;
?>
<?php
print “Hello World!”, “How are you?”;
?>
```

The echo code will be successfully sent to the client, but the print code will bring up a syntax error due to the unexpected comma (,) and the additional parameter or value after it. Though, if you want to use print with multiple parameters, you can concatenate the values of the parameters instead. String concatenation will be discussed later.

```
<?php
$x = 1 + print("test");
echo $x;
?>
<?php
$x = 1 + echo("test");
echo $x;
?>
```

The variable $x will have a value of 2 since the expression print("test") will return a value of 1. Also, even it is used as a value in an expression, the print command will still produce an output.

On the other hand, the echo version of the code will return a syntax error due to the unexpected appearance of echo in the expression.

Many web developers use the echo and print commands to provide dynamic web content for small and simple projects. In advanced projects, using return to send an array of variables that contain HTML content and displaying them using JavaScript or any client side scripting is a much better method.

Variables

Creating a variable in JavaScript requires you to declare it and use the keyword var. In PHP, you do not need to declare to create a variable. All you need to do is assign a value in a variable for it to be created. Also, variables in PHP always starts with a dollar sign ($).

```
<?php
$examplevariable = "Hello World!";
echo $examplevariable;
?>
```

There are rules to follow when creating a variable, which are similar to JavaScript's variable syntax.

- The variable's name or identifier must start with a dollar sign ($).
- An underscore or a letter must follow it.

- Placing a number or any symbol after the dollar sign instead will return a syntax error.
- The identifier must only contain letters, numbers, or underscores.
- Identifiers are case sensitive. The variable $x is treated differently from $X.

You can assign any type of data into a PHP variable. You can store strings, integers, floating numbers, and so on. If you have experienced coding using other programming languages, you might be thinking where you would need to declare the data type of the variable. You do not need to do that. PHP will handle that part for you. All you need to do is to assign the values in your variables.

Variable Scopes

Variables in PHP also change their scope, too, depending on the location where you created them.

Local

If you create a variable inside a function, it will be treated as a local variable. Unlike JavaScript, assigning a value to variable for the first time inside a function will not make them global due to way variables are created in PHP.

Global

If you want to create global variables, you can do it by creating a value outside your script's functions. Another method is to use the global keyword. The global keyword can let you create or access global variables inside a function. For example:

```
<?php
function test() {
	global $x;
	$x = "Hello World!";
}
test();
echo $x;
?>
```

In the example above, the line global $x defined variable $x as a global variable. Because of that, the echo command outside the function was able to access $x without encountering an undefined variable error.

As mentioned a while ago, you can use the global keyword to access global variables inside functions. Below is an example:

```
<?php
$x = "Hello Word!";
function test() {
	global $x;
	echo $x;
}
test();
?>
```

Just like before, the command echo will not encounter an error as long as the global keyword was used for the variable $x.

Another method you can use is to access your script's global values array, $GLOBALS. With $GLOBALS, you can create or access global values. Here is the previous example used once again, but with the $GLOBALS array used instead of the global keyword:

```
<?php
function test() {
	$GLOBALS['x'] = "Hello World!";
}
test();
echo $x;
?>
```

Take note that when using $GLOBALS, you do not need the dollar sign when creating or accessing a variable.

Static

If you are not comfortable in using global variables just to keep the values that your functions use, you can opt to convert your local variables to static. Unlike local variables, static variables are not removed from the memory once the function that houses them ends. They will stay in the memory like global variables, but they will be only accessible on the functions they reside in. For example:

```
<?php
```

```
function test() {
    static $y = 1;
    if (empty($y))
        {$y = 1;}
    echo $y . " ";
    $y += $y;
}
test();
test();
test();
test();
test();
?>
```

In the example, the variable $y's value is expected to grow double as the function is executed. With the help of static keyword, the existence and value of $y is kept in the script even if the function where it serves as a local variable was already executed.

As you can see, together with the declaration that the variable $y is static, the value of 1 was assigned to it. The assignment part in the declaration will only take effect during the first time the function was called and the static declaration was executed.

Superglobals

PHP has predefined global variables. They contain values that are commonly accessed, define, and manipulated in everyday server side data execution. Instead of manually capturing those values, PHP has placed them into its predefined superglobals to make the life of PHP programmers easier.

- **$GLOBALS**
- **$_SERVER**
- **$_REQUEST**
- **$_POST**
- **$_GET**
- **$_FILES**

- **$_ENV**
- **$_COOKIE**
- **$_SESSION**

SUPERGLOBALS HAVE **CORE USES IN PHP SCRIPTING. YOU WILL BE MOSTLY USING ONLY FIVE OF THESE SUPERGLOBALS IN YOUR EARLY DAYS IN CODING PHP. THEY ARE: $GLOBALS, $_SERVER, $_REQUEST, $_POST, AND $_GET.**

Constants

Constants are data storage containers just like variables, but they have global scope and can be assigned a value once. Also, the method of creating a constant is much different than creating a variable. When creating constants, you will need to use the define() construct. For example:

```
<?php
define(this_is_a_constant, “the value”, false);
?>
```

The define() construct has three parameters: define(name of constant, value of the constant, is case sensitive?). A valid constant name must start with a letter or an underscore – you do not need to place a dollar sign ($) before it. Aside from that, all other naming rules of variables apply to constants.

The third parameter requires a Boolean value. If the third parameter was given a true argument, constants can be accessed regardless of their case or capitalization. If set to false, its case will be strict. By default, it will be set to false.

Operators

By time, you must be already familiar with operators, so this book will only refresh you about them. Fortunately, the usage of operators in JavaScript and PHP is almost similar.

- Arithmetic: +, -, *, /, %, and **.
- Assignment: =, +=, -=, *=, /=, and %=.
- Comparison: ==, ===, !=, <>, !==, >, <, >=, and <=.

- Increment and Decrement: ++x, x++, --x, and x--.
- Logical: and, or, xor, &&, ||, and !.
- String: . and .=.
- Array: +, ==, ===, !=, <>, and !==.

Chapter 3: Flow Control

Flow control is needed when advancing or creating complex projects with any programming language. With them, you can control the blocks of statements that will be executed in your script or program. Most of the syntax and rules in the flow control constructs in PHP are almost similar to JavaScript, so you will not have a hard time learning to use them in your scripts.

Functions

Along the way, you will need to create functions for some of the frequently repeated procedures in your script. Creating functions in PHP is similar to JavaScript. The difference is that function names in PHP are not case sensitive. For example:

```
<?php
function test($parameter = "no argument input") {
	print $parameter;
}
TEST("Success!");
tEsT();
?>
```

In JavaScript, calling a function using its name in different casing will cause an error. With PHP, you will encounter no problems or errors as long as the spelling of the name is correct.

Also, did you notice the variable assignment on the sample function's parameter? The value assigned to the parameter's purpose is to provide a default value to it when the function was called without any arguments being passed for the parameter.

In the example, the second invocation of the function test did not provide any arguments for the function to assign to the $parameter. Because of that, the value 'no argument input' was assigned to $parameter instead.

In JavaScript, providing a default value for a parameter without any value can be tricky and long depending on the number of parameters that will require default arguments or parameter values.

Of course, just like JavaScript, PHP functions also return values with the use of the return keyword.

If, Else, and Elseif Statements

PHP has the same if construct syntax as JavaScript. To create an if block, start by typing the if keyword, and then follow it with an expression to be evaluated inside parentheses. After that, place the statements for your if block inside curly braces. Below is an example:

```
<?php
$color1 = "blue";
if ($color1 == "blue") {
	echo "The color is blue! Yay!";
}
?>
```

If you want your if statement to do something else if the condition returns a false, you can use else.

```
<?php
$color1 = "blue";
if ($color1 == "blue") {
	echo "The color is blue! Yay!";
}
else {
	echo "The color is not blue, you liar!";
}
?>
```

In case you want to check for more conditions in your else statements, you can use elseif instead nesting an if statement inside else. For example:

```
<?php
$color1 = "blue";
if ($color1 == "blue") {
	echo "The color is blue! Yay!";
}
else {
	if ($color == "green") {
		echo "Hmm. I like green, too. Yay!";
	}
	else {
```

```
            echo "The color is not blue, you liar!";
        }
}
?>
```

Is the same as:

```
<?php
$color1 = "blue";
if ($color1 == "blue") {
        echo "The color is blue! Yay!";
}
elseif ($color == "green" {
        echo "Hmm. I like green, too. Yay!";}
else {
        echo "The color is not blue, you liar!";
}
?>
```

Using elseif is less messy and is easier to read.

Switch Statement

However, if you are going to check for multiple conditions for one expression or variable and place a lot of statements per condition satisfied, it is better to use switch than if statements. For example, the previous if statement is the same as:

```
<?php
$color1 = "blue";
switch ($color1) {
        case "blue":
                echo "The color is blue! Yay!";
                break;
        case "green":
                echo "Hmm. I like green, too. Yay!";
                break;
        case default:
                echo "The color is not blue, you liar!";
}
?>
```

The keyword switch starts the switch statement. Besides it is the value or expression that you will test. It must be enclosed in parentheses.

Every case keyword entry must be accompanied with the value that you want to compare against the expression being tested. Each case statement can be translated as if <expression 1> is equal to <expression 2>, and then perform the statements below.

The break keyword is used to signal the script that the case block is over and the any following statements after it should not be done.

On the other hand, the default case will be executed when no case statements were satisfied by the expression being tested.

Chapter 4: Data Types – Part 1

PHP also has the same data types that you can create and use in other programming languages. Some of the data types in PHP have different ways of being created and assigned from the data types in JavaScript.

Strings

Any character or combination of characters placed in double or single quotes are considered strings in PHP. In PHP, you will deal with text a lot more often than other programming languages. PHP is used typically to handle data going from the client to the server and vice versa. Due to that, you must familiarize yourself with a few of the most common used string operators and methods.

Numbers

Integer

Integers are whole numbers without fractional components or values after the decimal value. When assigning or using integers in PHP, it is important that you do not place blanks and commas between them to denote or separate place values.

An integer value can be positive, negative or zero. In PHP, you can display integers in three forms: decimal (base 10), octal (base 8), or hexadecimal (base 16). To denote that a value is in hexadecimal form, always put the prefix 0x (zero-x) with the value (e.g., 0x1F, 0x4E244D, 0xFF11AA). On the other hand, to denote that a value is in octal form, put the prefix 0 (zero) with the value (e.g., 045, 065, and 0254).

If you echo or print an integer variable, its value will be automatically presented in its decimal form. In case that you want to show it in hexadecimal or octal you can use dechex() or decoct() respectively. For example:

```
<?php
echo dechex(255);
echo decoct(9);
?>
```

The first echo will return FF, which is 255 in decimal. The second echo will return 11, which is 9 in octal. As you might have noticed, the prefix 0x and 0 were not present in the result. The prefixes only apply when you write those two presentations of integers in your script.

On the other hand, you can use hexdec() to reformat a hexadecimal value to decimal and use octdec() to reformat an octal value to decimal.

You might think of converting hex to oct or vice versa. Unfortunately, PHP does not have constructs like hexoct() or octhex(). To perform that kind of operation, you will need to manually convert the integer to decimal first then convert it to hex or oct.

Float or Double

Floating numbers are real numbers (or approximations of real numbers). In other words, it can contain fractional decimal values.

Since integers are a subset of real numbers, integers are floating numbers. Just adding a decimal point and a zero to an integer in PHP will make PHP consider that the type of the variable that will store that value is float instead of integer.

Boolean

Boolean is composed of two values: True and False. In PHP, true and false are not case sensitive. Both values are used primarily in conditional statements, just like in JavaScript.

Also, false is equivalent to null, a blank string, and 0 while true is equivalent to any number except 0 or any string that contains at least one character.

NULL

This is a special value type. In case that a variable does not contain a value from any other data types, it will have a NULL value instead. For example, if you try to access a property from an object that has not been assigned a value yet, it will have a NULL value. By the way, you can assign NULL to variables, too.

Resource

RESOURCES IS A SPECIAL VARIABLE TYPE. THEY ONLY SERVE AS A REFERENCE TO EXTERNAL RESOURCE AND ARE ONLY CREATED BY SPECIAL FUNCTIONS. AN EXAMPLE OF A RESOURCE IS A DATABASE LINK.

Chapter 5: Data Types – Part 2

The data types explained in this chapter are essential to your PHP programming life. In other programming languages, you can live without this data types. However, in PHP, you will encounter them most of the time, especially if you will start to learn and use databases on your scripts.

ARRAYS

Arrays are data containers for multiple values. You can store numbers, strings, and even arrays in an array. Array in PHP is a tad different in JavaScript, so it will be discussed in detail in this book.

There are three types of array in PHP: indexed, associative, and multidimensional.

Indexed Arrays

Indexed array is the simplest form of arrays in PHP. For those people who are having a hard time understanding arrays, think of an array as a numbered list that starts with zero. To create or assign values to an array, you must use the construct array(). For example:

```
<?php
$examplearray = array(1, 2, "three");
?>
```

To call values inside an array, you must call them using their respective indices. For example:

```
<?php
$examplearray = array(1, 2, "three");
echo $examplearray[0];
echo $examplearray['2'];
?>
```

The first echo will reply with 1 and the second echo will reply three. As you can see, in indexed arrays, you can call values with just a number or a number inside quotes. When dealing with indexed arrays, it is best that you use the first method.

Since the number 1 was the first value to be assigned to the array, index 0 was assigned to it. The index number of the values in an array increment by 1. So, the index numbers of the values 2 and three are 1 and 2 respectively.

Associative Arrays

The biggest difference between associative arrays and indexed arrays is that you can define the index keys of the values in associative arrays. The variable $GLOBALS is one of the best example of associative arrays in PHP. To create an associative array, follow the example:

```
<?php
$examplearray = array("indexo" => "John", 2 => "Marci");
echo $examplearray["indexo"];
echo $examplearray[2];
?>
```

The first echo will return John and the second echo will return Marci. Take note that if you use associative array, the values will not have indexed numbers.

Multidimensional Arrays

Multidimensional arrays can store values, indexed arrays, and associative arrays. If you create an array in your script, the $GLOBALS variable will become a multidimensional array. You can insert indexed or associative arrays in multidimensional arrays. However, take note that the same rules apply to their index keys. To create one, follow the example below:

```
<?php
$examplearray = array(array("test1", 1, 2), array("test2" =>
3, "test3" => 4), array("test4", 5, 6));
echo $examplearray[1]["test2"];
echo $examplearray[1][1];
echo $examplearray[2][0];
?>
```

As you can see, creating multidimensional arrays is just like nesting arrays on its value. Calling values from multidimensional is simple.

If a value was assigned, it can be called like a regular array value using its index key. If a value was paired with a named key, it can be called by its name. If an array was assigned, you can call the value inside it by calling the index key of the array first, and then the index key of the value inside it.

In the example, the third echo called the array in index 2 and accessed the value located on its 0 index. Hence, it returned test4.

Objects

Objects are like small programs inside your script. You can assign variables within them called properties. You can also assign functions within them called methods.

Creating and using objects can make you save hundreds of lines of code, especially if you have some bundle of codes that you need to use repeatedly on your scripts. To be on the safe side, the advantages of using objects depend on the situation and your preferences.

Debates about using objects in their scripts (object oriented programming) or using functions (procedural programming) instead have been going on forever. It is up to you if you will revolve your programs around objects or not.

Nevertheless, to create objects, you must create a class for them first. Below is an example on how to create a class in PHP.

```
<?php
class Posts {
	function getPost() {
		$this->post1 = "Post Number 1.";
	}
	var $post2 = "Post Number 2.";
}

$test = new Posts();
echo $test->post2;
$test->getPost();
echo $test->post1;
?>
```

In this example, a new class was created using the class keyword. The name of the class being created is Posts. In class declarations, you can create functions that will be methods for the objects under the class. And you can create variables that will be properties for the subjects under the class.

First, a function was declared. If the function was called, it will create a property for an object under the Posts class called post1. Also, a value was assigned to it. You might have noticed the $this part in the declaration inside the function. The $this variable represents the object that owns the function being declared.

Besides it is a dash and a chevron (->). Some programmers informally call it as the instance operator. This operator allows access to the instances (methods and properties) of an object. In the statement, the script is accessing the post1 property inside the $this object, which is the object that owns the function. After accessing the property, the statement assigned a value to it.

Aside from the function or method declaration, the script created a property called post2, which is a variable owned by the Posts class. To declare one, you need to use the keyword var (much like in JavaScript). After this statement, the class declaration ends.

The next statement contains the variable assignment, $test = new Posts(). Technically, that means that the variable $test will become a new object under the Posts class. All the methods and properties that was declared inside the Posts() class declaration will be given to it.

To test if the $test class became a container for a Posts object, the script accessed the property post2 from $test and then echoed it to produce an output. The echo will return , 'Post number 2.'. Indeed, the $test variable is already an object under the Posts class.

What if you call and print the property post1 from the variable $test? It will not return anything since it has not been created or initialized yet. To make it available, you need to invoke the getPost() method of $test. Once you do, you will be able to access the property post1.

And that is just the tip of the iceberg. You will be working more on objects on advanced PHP projects.

Conclusion

Thank you again for purchasing this book!

I hope this book was able to help you to learn PHP fast.

The next step is to:

Learn the other superglobals

Learn from handling in HTML, JavaScript, and PHP

Learn using MySQL

Finally, if you enjoyed this book, please take the time to share your thoughts and post a review on Amazon. We do our best to reach out to readers and provide the best value we can. Your positive review will help us achieve that. It'd be greatly appreciated!

Thank you and good luck!

Check Out My Other Books

Below you'll find some of my other popular books that are popular on Amazon and Kindle as well. Simply click on the links below to check them out. Alternatively, you can visit my author page on Amazon to see other work done by me.

Android Programming in a Day

Python Programming in a Day

C Programming Success in a Day

CSS Programming Professional Made Easy

C Programming Professional Made Easy

JavaScript Programming Made Easy

Windows 8 Tips for Beginners

Windows 8 Tips for Beginners

HTML Professional Programming Made Easy

Programming Box Set #81: Android Programming in a Day & PHP Programming Professional Made Easy

C ++ Programming Success in a Day

If the links do not work, for whatever reason, you can simply search for these titles on the Amazon website to find them.